God's Last Day's People

Mel Bond (Oyate Obmanpi)

Unless otherwise indicated all Scripture quotations are taken from the King James Version of the Bible or Prominent Hebrew and Greek Concordances.

GOD'S LAST DAY'S PEOPLE
Copyright 2007 by Rev. Mel Bond
140 N. Point Prairie Rd.
Wentzville, MO 63385

Editor: Stephen Deutschmann
7 Carnac Ct., Lake St. Louis, MO 63367

Printed in the United States of America
All rights reserved under International Copyright Law. Contents and/or cover may not be reproduced in whole or in part in any form without the express written consent of the Publisher

ISBN 1-882318-05-6

DEDICATION

I dedicate this book to my father and my mother (Elven and Anna Marie Bond (Bray) who I love and thank so much for teaching me the most powerful, most important things of life. They taught me about unconditional love, forgiveness, and giving. They taught me about God.

Theresa Stead 4/4 Lakota

ENDORSEMENT

Many individuals filled with the HOLY SPIRIT have spoken about the BROWN sleeping GIANT. The time has come for GOD to start the awakening of that GIANT. The Lakota people that are filled with the HOLY GHOST are ready to stand and fight the spiritual war.

Robert & Theresa Stead
White Horse Ministry
PO Box 903
Mission, SD 57555
(605) 856-4699
nunpa@msn.com

Mike Pahsetopah
Osage, Cherokee, Yuchi, Creek

ENDORSEMENT

This book really touched my heart and fueled my spirit. Mel reveals a message that is simple, informative, and clearly describes God's last day's people.

I encourage everyone that is hungry and thirsty to read this book.

Mike Pahsetopah
Bible Faith Native American Ministry
2834 South Hickory Street
Sapulpa, Oklahoma 74066
918-224-2442
EagleWings3@Cox.net

CONTENTS

              Introduction 1

CHAPTER 1 Indians Are Strong People 5

CHAPTER 2 Indians Are Visionaries 11

CHAPTER 3 Indians Know How To Die 25

CHAPTER 4 Big Forgivers 29

CHAPTER 5 Humility 37

CHAPTER 6 Indians Are Givers 43

CHAPTER 7 Indians Are People Of Integrity 51

INTRODUCTION

Why God Wants To Use American Indians For His Last Day's Work

Blow the trumpet! A great and strong people; there hath not been ever like them, neither shall there be any more! Nothing shall escape them! (Joel 2:1-3)

Scripturally, God needs a people to usher in the ministry of Signs and Wonders, as spelled out plainly in Joel 2.

God has always chosen a special *people* to become the leaders during each biblical time period. The last days will be no exception, and will be a time of the greatest manifestations of God's power; greater than has ever existed on the earth. He will use a people that exhibit the special Godly qualities that American Indians have. Although people of other races have these qualities, the percentage in the American Indian population is much higher. I believe that is why the entire American Indian population was nearly destroyed. It is possible that satan knew American Indians were to become the chosen people to usher in the last days and the rapture. By destroying all, or most all American Indians, God's plan for the last days could be stopped. However, satan did not succeed! We were nearly destroyed, but now we are very much alive and growing.

I believe God wants to use American Indians, **and like minded people**, to usher in the last day's final movement which will bring in the last great harvest spoken of in Revelations 4:6; 5:9; 13, and usher in the rapture of the Church (I Thessalonians 4:15-18). This book will reveal the qualities required of leaders to become that strong, mighty people. God's Signs and Wonders will flow freely from the hearts of these people.

So there is no misunderstanding, I want to make something clear, right up front. It is my strong perception that God is going to use American Indians, **and like minded people,** to become the leaders for the last day's harvest. As you read this book, please remember, when I am talking about American Indians, I am also talking about other people that are like minded. I am not attempting to promote American Indians above other people. Maybe you can understand my heart by this illustration: Some people are born to sing and they sing very well. That is not to say that other people can not learn to be good singers. But for people that are born to sing, singing always comes easier.

I have learned that American Indians use a portion of their brain that causes them to be more spiritually minded than most other people. Being more spiritually minded does not mean we are better than any one else. Just as a gifted singer, musician, carpenter, artist, or any other gifted person, is not better than any one else. Again, I want to make it clear, I know that other people are also born with these qualities, I just see them more prevalent among American Indians than other people.

I have traveled to 27 different countries all over the world, and some of these countries I have visited as many as 15 times. Some of the people in these countries are spiritually minded. It is just my observation and perception that American Indians are one of the most spiritually minded people that God desires to use to usher in the last day's Signs and Wonders, and bring to His heavenly kingdom the greatest number of people ever. The good news is that other people can learn these qualities.

As you study this book, you will see that all of these qualities fall under the character of holiness. In Romans 1:4, Jesus was declared ordained by God in the highest manner, to be the Son of God, with miracle working power, according to the Spirit of Holiness! Jesus is coming for a glorious Church. The word *glorious* is a people with the very *reputation of God.* I John 3:2…….. WE KNOW, (not think so, or hope so) that when HE shall appear, WE SHALL BE LIKE HIM!

I pray this book will awaken the sleeping army (AMERICAN INDIANS) and like minded people.

CHAPTER 1

Indians Are Strong People

In Joel chapter 2, the Scripture is plain in talking about a last day's army that will usher in the last day's Signs and Wonders. This last day's people that are used in the ministry of Signs and Wonders is referred to by God as His army (Joel 2:11; 25). An army is a strong people, a people equipped to conquer areas that other people can not conquer. In Joel 2:2, God's Word says that the last day's people ministering Signs and Wonders will be a great and strong (powerful) people. There have never been a people like these, and neither shall there be any more like them. In verse 3, God says *nothing* shall escape them! Keep in mind that the Scriptures say *nothing* shall escape them. Plainly, sickness, disease, incurable situations, deafness, blindness, deformity and physical death are things that shall not escape them. Nothing means *nothing*!

INDIANS HAVE STRONG WILLS

A people of this caliber are a people having a strongly fixed mind. A people of this caliber are a people of strong wills. When this kind of people gets their will in 100% agreement with God's will, you have a people that are more destructive to satan and his kingdom than any people that have ever walked the earth.

My father was an American Indian. I lived with and saw this type of will exercised in my father's life. It did not matter what people said to him or did to him, if he did not want to do something, he was not for sale. It was not possible to scare my father with the greatest of threats. If he did not want to do something, he was not going to do it.

This strong will is something that we Indian people are born with. It does not matter how much money is offered, if we do not want to do something, we will not do it. We can not be bought! We can be beaten, threatened, or intimidated in any way imaginable; however, if our will is against it, we will not do it.

When the Europeans first settled in America, they unsuccessfully tried to make slaves of Indians. They beat us unmercifully, but we would still not do their work. They would kill our people in front of us, to get us to do their work, and we still refused. Indians have extremely strong will power.

On the other hand, if Indians believe in something we want to do, we will gladly work beyond reason. We will sacrifice beyond natural reasoning to accomplish what we believe in. We will gladly die for what we believe in. This is the type of strength God needs in a people to perform Signs and Wonders across the world to win the masses to the Lord.

INDIANS HAVE INDEPENDENT PERSONALITIES

Indians do not need anyone or anything to help us. We have the belief that we can do it all by ourselves. Of course, this type of character is wrong and dangerous if satan uses it. However, if this type of strong personality is used by the Lord, satan is going to look for new places to hide. When this type of mighty people (the Indians and like minded people) renew their minds with God's Word (Romans 12:1, 2), and find out that they can do ALL THINGS THROUGH CHRIST who strengthens us, a powerful people come into existence.

When I was 18 years old I owned a 1966 Ford Mustang. This automobile meant very much to me. I was in the military at that time, stationed at Fort Riley, Kansas. At that time, I felt quite alone. I felt like that Mustang was my best friend (except for Jesus). I spent a lot of time maintaining and cleaning the car. One evening I drove the car up on a ramp to change the oil. I accidentally drove my car off the side of the ramp and the car hung in the air, with one tire on the ramp and the other front tire off the ramp. When I realized my dilemma, I immediately began to cry out to the Lord. I knew if I had to leave the car there over night, it would most likely be vandalized. When I cried out to the Lord, immediately Philippians 4:13 came strongly into my mind. In those years, I did not have anyone to feed me doubt and unbelief, and tell me that strong, literal passages of the Bible meant something different. I simply believed the Bible meant what it said. I believed it not only meant spiritual strength, but also physical strength. So, just like Samson, I put my hands on the bottom of the car and picked it up with my arms. No human on this earth can do that. But an Indian mind, which has been renewed by God's Word, believes he or she can do ALL things with God's strength working through them.

Indians that have their minds renewed by God's Word are not dependent upon this world's system. They are not dependent upon man's system or approval. They are not dependent upon medical science, and are not dependent upon this world's financial system. We acquire greater independence than we have ever had. This type of independence, the type our hearts cry deeply for, is only found when we fully depend upon the Lord and His unfailing promises.

INDIANS DO NOT CARE WHAT OTHERS THINK

Indians are strongly focused on our goals, regardless of what the rest of the world thinks. We are not followers, we are leaders. Leaders are strong people that adventure into areas that no other people would remotely consider. We are not interested in trying to impress people. We do not care what the rest of the world is wearing. We will gladly wear something that we've made, and believe we are dressed fine. We are not afraid of being laughed at for being different. In fact, we are independently minded; we are not comfortable unless we are different. I again want to say, all of these qualities are horrible if satan uses them. But we become champion of champions when God uses these qualities.

WE ARE PEOPLE OF HONOR

Indians do not break our ranks at any cost (Joel 2:7). When you become our friend, we will lay down our lives to help you. We will not talk one way in front of your face, and then another way when you are not around. We will not hurt others with our words, especially those that we are at war with us. We would not do anything that would be of harm to them (Neither shall one thrust another v.8). No matter what you do to an Indian, you can not get them to speak against another. This is a mark of a strong character.

When this quality of strength, power and might is used by God, based upon His Word, satan's kingdom of the land shall tremble (Joel 2:1). Jesus said in Matthew 22:37 that the greatest commandment of all is to Love the Lord thy God with all of your heart and mind. Jesus said in verse 39 that the second commandment is like the first. The second commandment is to love your neighbor as yourself. If you will not even speak a bad report behind closed doors about your neighbor, you are in the highest degree of loving your neighbor as Jesus mentioned. Jesus also said in the next verse, that upon these two commandments hang all of God's commandments. (This means all of the Scriptures, and all of God's laws and promises.) It takes a strong people to have all of these qualities, and Indians have all of these qualities.

Nothing shall escape these strong people. Every person will know of God's goodness, greatness and powerfulness (v.3). Every demonic work in the earth shall quake before them; the spiritual wickedness in high places shall tremble (v.10). In Joel 2:7, it says these strong people shall not break their ranks. When people will not give a bad report about another in secret, a powerful display of unity is shown. God said in Genesis 11:6 that an ungodly people would be able to do anything they could imagine because of unity. Today we have a new covenant, established upon better and greater promises. So, how much more is this law of God's unity going to work for Indian people in these final last days, when we will not break our ranks? Our imagination will be the only limit to everything God's Word says we are and can do. We will raise the dead, open the blinded eyes, and open the deaf ears, all for the purpose of winning the last day's great harvest.

CHAPTER 2

Indians Are Visionaries

Indians are seers. Our biological make up is the foundation for being seers, visionaries.

This chapter is the heart of the book. I could easily devote 300 pages to this subject. However, I want to focus on the mandate, and not excess.

American Indians use a part of their brain that most other people do not use. This portion of the brain allows us to see, feel, hear, smell, and taste in the spirit world. This does not mean we are better than any one else. Swiss people are born to make good watches. You would not want a watch that I would make. Does that mean Swiss people are better? Of course they are not better. Each nationality has special gifts and talents that they were born with.

In 1890, Chief Sitting Bull announced to agent McLaughlin, "I AM AN INDIAN; GOD ALMIGHTY MADE ME AN INDIAN"! Agent McLaughlin was trying to get Chief Sitting Bull to conform to the European white culture.

God made us all different so we could appreciate and need each other. People who are born with a natural talent can teach other people their talent. For instance, someone who is born with the natural talent to play a musical instrument makes a very good teacher of that musical instrument. The student who was not born with the natural talent to play that musical instrument may never become as good as the teacher, but may become very good through many hours of devoted practice.

In a like manner, Indians can teach others how to flow with their God given talents. In this book, every one can learn how to use these God given Indian talents and be used of God in a great way. The following paragraphs describe some of these important talents.

MENTAL VISIONS

A mental vision is a vision that anyone can have anytime. This vision is seen in the mind because it has been seen previously in the natural (with human eyes), or the individual's mind has been given knowledge which makes it easy to have a mental picture. Anyone can experience a mental vision at will.

In the Indian mind however, we see things in our minds in a more supernatural way. For example, it is easy for us to see ourselves doing something that is not natural. Our ancestors may have seen themselves killing a buffalo with primitive weapons. Today, we may see ourselves accomplishing goals which other humans can not accomplish. Even if we do not accomplish our goals, we feel that we will the next time we try.

The Indian mind can easily have mental pictures of the supernatural. It is very normal for Indians to think supernatural. We are spiritually minded. For example, I described in Chapter 1 the time when I drove my 1966 Ford Mustang off the side of a ramp. When I was under my car, I had a mental picture of me picking the car up with God's strength, and then I did it in the natural. It was not an attempt to impress anyone. The time was late at night and no one was within two blocks of my location. Before I was a Christian, I would have believed I could lift the car, and I would have failed. However, after becoming a Christian and having read the Bible through at least 6 times, I had a mental picture of lifting that car because Philippians 4:13 came to my mind ["I am able to do all things through the one (Christ) who strengthens me."]. I not only had a mental vision of doing the supernatural, but I had an infallible foundation from Almighty God for my mental vision.

The purpose of having our minds renewed with God's Word is to enable us to have mental pictures of God's Word being accomplished through us. (If our minds are not renewed with God's Word, we will think and see visions which are not Scriptural, and not for God's glory.) The Indian mind thinks and sees in the supernatural so deeply that the average person would think it is foolish. However to us Indians, it is very real. When we put God's Word in our minds, we can easily see ourselves doing the works of Jesus and greater (John 14:12-14). In one gathering, I used to see myself before thousands of people, opening blinded eyes, deaf ears, raising the dead, and getting thousands of people saved and filled with the Holy Spirit. I purposely enjoyed day dreaming about these supernatural things, even though it was totally impossible and only a dream. Now, God works through me to perform these acts whenever I want.

From a Scriptural standpoint, the most important kind of a vision is a mental vision. Proverbs 29:18 gives the best description of a mental vision. "Where there is no vision, the people perish. But he that keepeth the law, happy is he." Notice that the word *vision*, and *keepeth the law*, is used interchangeably. Plainly, God is telling us that we can have visions by keeping the law (which is His Word), and then we will be happy. The word *vision* in this verse has a fuller meaning. It also means to *mentally have a dream, especially to have a vision, mentally dream an oracle, revelation, or bind firmly.*

The strongest mandate of God is an oracle. An oracle is the highest, strongest words, command, appointment, purpose, work, and power of God. All of these terms are straight from the Hebrew word for *oracle*. When we Indians (or like minded people) take God's Word and purposely have a mental vision, we are having God's Divine oracle in the highest order of God's mind and purpose.

I've been to several countries doing miracle and healing crusades. When I see deformed people, I initiate a vision. I mentally see myself taking hold of their deformed bodies and straightening them out. I pray for them in a very tender and soft way, releasing God's anointing as Jesus instructed me in a vision. If I do not see the natural manifestation, I act out what I just purposely visualized. I grab the arm, leg, foot, or whatever it is, and straighten it out in Jesus' name. The deformed body becomes straight and healed in the natural.

I see myself and others doing all of the miracles described in the Bible. These miracles include raising the dead corpse to life again, opening rivers and seas, then walking through the midst of rivers and seas on dry ground, and making the sun and the moon to stand still for at least a day or two. All of these Scriptural, supernatural miracles were done in the Bible, and all in the first month of the last season, just before the rapture (Joel 2:23, 28). Performing these miracles validate to an ungodly world that there is ONLY ONE ALMIGHTY GOD, and He can give them a greater miracle than all of these supernatural manifestations. We will then have the world's undivided attention to say, "A greater miracle is living forever, and all who read and follow Romans 10:9, 10, shall live forever". The miracles will produce millions of the most beautiful, most powerful sermons ever preached. God must have a people who see in, and experience, the spirit world in order to fulfill His last day's agenda.

Another example of Indians in the 19th century validates the God given ability to be a seer. A great Lakota Sioux man by the name of Charles Eastman (Ohiyesa) was the doctor for the survivors of the Wounded Knee Massacre on December 29, 1890. Eastman says things like, "Nothing is too miraculous, or beyond the thinking of, the Indian mind". The Indian mind is not surprised of a donkey talking (Numbers 22:25-27) or for the sun and moon to stand still (Joshua 10:12-14). All things are simple for the great Creator to do, say the Indian mind.

OPEN VISIONS

The Greek word for this *open vision* is "Op'tom'ahee". This vision means to gaze at something in your natural alertness, with your natural eyes wide open, seeing something supernatural and remarkable.

For as long as I can remember, I have been able to see into the spirit world often (having "Op'tom'ahee" visions). The Indian mind is open to the spirit world and we believe in it with our whole heart. We are very conscious of the spirit world throughout our lives. Since open visions can be both good and bad, I never ask for them, and as a boy, never wanted to experience them.

My dad was in World War II, serving as an Army Infantry man. I found out from my mother that he fought in 5 of the largest, worst battles of the war. My mother also told me that he received a Purple Heart for being wounded in battle, and received a few other medals for actions unknown to us. Not until after he passed away on August 13, 2004, did I find out that he was honored with 4 Bronze Stars. I contacted the Veteran's Administration, and they gave me duplicates of his medals and some documents of his military affairs. All of the years I knew my dad (as he and my brother were my best male friends), he never mentioned anything about his bravery in the military. In fact, I know very little of what he did, since he would never talk about it. He would always change the subject when his military career came up in conversation. This is another great characteristic of the American Indian; they will never talk or brag about their accomplishments. You can be sitting next to one of the greatest Indian persons on the face of the earth, and you would think you are sitting by the most common person on the earth. The humility of God Almighty rules in the heart of the American Indian.

The Indian who has not been born again, and not renewed

his mind with God's Word, is not afraid of anything, man or beast. He or she will fight a full grown buffalo, and believe they will win the fight by themselves. However, to get that same Indian to walk down a dark, lonely road at night will take a lot of convincing. Indians are afraid that the spirit world may jump on them. Indians also know you can not fight a spirit with any amount of natural strength and ability. Once an Indian gets saved, they must spend a lot of time learning that they have authority over the devil and demons. Since Indians can see devils and demons, we know they are real. You might say Indians are spooky! We are, until we get saved!

God needs a people that can go into the spirit world and fight. Go into the spirit world and take back what God has given us. Go into the Spirit world and receive God's anointing to do the works of Jesus. Go into the Spirit world and talk to Jesus concerning His Word.

An elderly Lakota Pastor friend of mine, living on the Rosebud Sioux Indian Reservation, told me this story many years ago. He said he went to the Antelope Restaurant one morning, and sat down by a well known medicine man. The medicine man told him about a person that came to him, and paid him to put a curse on a family. The medicine man said he waited until one evening, and then he traveled by spirit (his spirit got out of his body) down the road toward the people's home. He said the closer he got to the home, the more he saw a powerful light that shined out of every crack of the house. The light shined out of the windows, under the doors, etc. The medicine man said the light tormented him. He said he covered his eyes and face, as much as he possibly could, and tried to get as close to the house as he could.

However, he said he knew he could not put the curse upon the family because of the powerful light that was inside of the house. The light was so powerful it radiated out of the windows, cracks, and under the door. He decided he would try to get as close to a window as he could, to at least see what was producing this powerful light that was hindering and tormenting him. The medicine man said the family was on their knees praying. He noticed a couple from the Lakota Pastor's church, and they were leading this family to accept Jesus Christ as their Lord and Savior. The medicine man then told the Lakota Pastor, "If you Christians ever find out how much power you've got – we are ruined"!

When the Indian mind gets renewed with the greatest power in all of existence, with God's Word (Romans 12:1-30), they become not only spiritually minded, they become Godly inspired. They become just like Jesus. God needs a spiritually minded people that know the spirit world is more real than the natural world. God needs a spiritually minded people that will go into the spirit world and take Miracles and Healings, Signs and Wonders, that Jesus paid for, and bring them into the natural world. God needs a spiritually minded people that can see demonic activity and put a stop to them in Jesus' name (Philippians 2:5, 9). God needs a spiritually minded people that can see angels and work with them for God's glory.

The last day's army must be the most spiritually minded people that have ever existed. The season just before the rapture is going to be a time of the most supernatural manifestation of God's awesome power (Joel 2:23; I Peter 1:5). In my book titled "IF WE NEGLECT THE MINISTRY OF SIGNS AND WONDERS WE NEGLECT

THE RAPTURE", I have provided chapters of Scriptures which validate this point. This will be a time when the spirit world is activated to new heights. The sleeping giant (Indian people) are now rising to its God ordained position.

The hand of the Lord is now upon me. He is now setting me down in the midst of a nation full of bones that have been forgotten. The Lord asks me, "Can these bones live again?" Then He said unto me, "Prophesy to these bones", say to them, "O dry bones, hear the Word of the Lord". Thus saith the Lord, "These bones shall live again. I, the Lord God, will not only cause you to live again, but I will return unto you all that has been lost by the many generations before you. And you shall know that I am the Lord."

The Lord now tells me to Prophesy to the wind. "Come from the four corners and breathe upon these slain, that they may live. I see them now standing upon their feet, an exceedingly great army". Now, thus saith the Lord, "My Spirit shall come upon you, and you shall be turned into another person. When this happens, you will have the ability to do whatever the Spirit of the Lord and the Word of the Lord directs you to do. Indian people, you shall now be my last day's army, equipped with Signs and Wonders." For the prophecy the Lord just spoke through me (July 15, 2006, 8:26pm), read Ezekiel 37:1-10; I Samuel 10:6, 7.

To validate that Indians are born seers, please read documented material that was actually spoken by many of the great American Indians. Read material spoken by Wovoka, Short Bull, Kicking Bear, and Chief Joseph. I will attempt to give you a sampling of this material.

Wovoka was a Paiute Indian born about 1856. He was a spiritual leader who had an experience in which he died and went to heaven. While he was there, Jesus Christ gave him instructions for a dance, and a message of peace to share with all people. About the spring of 1890, approximately 1500 Indians, from several different tribes, traveled long distances to Wovoka's camp to learn about this dance, and its meaning. Among the Lakota Indians, the dance was known as Wanagi Wacapi which means "Spirit Dance" or "Ghost Dance". Today, it would be called the "Holy Ghost Dance". It was preformed by a circle of dancers, grasping each others hands tightly, swinging their arms back and forth, chanting Ghost Dance songs, all the while looking up to the heavens. They would dance earnestly for hours, with great fervent, and in desperation to get help from the Great Spirit (which they recognized as the Almighty God of the King James Bible). *Some worshipers would dance until they fell into unconsciousness and experience visions from God*. Many would go to heaven after falling under God's power. Sometimes, while in heaven, they would see their relatives and friends who had passed away.

At this time in American Indian history (early 1890's), the Indians where starving and freezing to death, primarily due to extremely poor living conditions, and very poor clothing and housing allotments. They were desperate to hear from God. The Indians danced, sang, and worshiped with their whole hearts.

Kicking Bear and Short Bull were very active "Ghost Dancers", and their thoughts are well documented in several publications. Short Bull was particularly active in teaching and preaching about the "Ghost Dance" and his words are in extreme agreement with the King James Bible. To paraphrase a statement made by Short Bull in 1906, he said, "Visions are usual among Indian people". On different occasions, Short Bull made statements similar to the following statements. "To visit the spirit-camp (going to Heaven) was probably a vision." "To the Indian, such an experience was just as real as being awake and having the same experience." "To visit the other camp (Heaven) was a reality". As you read publications describing Short Bull's experiences during the Ghost Dance, you will find him stating many times that he would fall to the ground and his spirit would go to Heaven. These experiences were so profound that they changed his character and the course of his life. Statements by these American Indians validate the seer gift with Indians.

DREAMS

In the Indian mind, there are dreams we have which are actual encounters in the spirit world. We believe with our whole heart that such dreams are actually experiencing the most real world, that is to say, the ***eternal spirit world***. Many times Indians, and even entire tribes, have changed the course of their lives because of the great confidence we have in dreams. Long before Indians ever saw or knew a white man, we believed Wakantanka (God Almighty) communicates His divine plans to us through visions.

Notice the strong Scriptural support in Job 33:14, 15, for this subject. "For God speaketh once, yea twice, yet man perceiveth it not". In verse 15, "In a dream, in a vision of the night, when deep sleep falleth upon men, in slumberings upon the bed; (verse 16) that he openeth the ears of men, and sealeth their instructions".

God's Word teaches us that He is speaking to us many times throughout our normal day. However, many times we get our days so full of the natural world, that we do not perceive or hear God's voice. So God waits until our flesh and mind are asleep, and then speaks directly to our spirits through dreams.

In the original language of the Bible, throughout the Scriptures, you will notice the words vision, dream, and trance all refer to the same experience. Occasionally, you will notice that a completely different word is used, with a major interpretation explaining the experience. As it is in all languages, many different words exist which refer to the exact same meaning. For example, in the English language, the word man, male, father, husband, and grandfather may all describe the exact same person.

God considers dreams as an extremely high order for communicating with humans. Jesus was, and is, the highest order of God toward humanity. Five times in the Scriptures, God gave humans dreams to save the life of Jesus. If the life of Jesus was destroyed before the appointed time, the highest purpose of God toward humanity would not have been fulfilled. Refer to the Scriptures of Matthew 1:20; 2:12, 13, 19, and 22. People in Biblical times believed in dreams, just like we Indians, and the highest order of God's will was established. The Indian people were convinced that Wakantanka was directly communicating with them.

If you look Scripturally at the words ***vision, dream, and trance,*** you will see that God comes to people in dreams. A few examples of Scriptures which validate this subject are Genesis 20:3, 6; 31:24, and I Kings 3:5.

In the American Indian culture, we craft dream catchers in various patterns, as an icon of great respect to God ordained dreams.

CHAPTER 3

Indians Know How To Die

Chief Crazy Horse, one of the greatest Sioux warriors of all time, is a powerful example of an American Indian dying to self. He received his name through his strong acts of self denial so others could have a better way of life. As a young man, Chief Crazy Horse would hunt for food to feed his people, and many times refrain from eating himself so that others would not go hungry.

As a young warrior, Chief Crazy Horse often positioned himself on a hilltop with a band of warriors. From this position, it was easy to spot approaching cavalry troops. Chief Crazy horse knew that if he rode out to the troops, to tease the enemy, he could draw them into an ambush with the remaining warriors. Chief Crazy Horse would instruct the warriors of his plan. Then, Crazy Horse would cry out HOKA HEY (TODAY IS A GOOD DAY TO DIE), and in a fearless act of bravery, would ride out to charge into the well armed cavalry troops. Crazy Horse was armed with only a bow and arrow, but he had the commitment of his whole heart. During all of the battles in which he demonstrated these acts of bravery and self denial, Crazy Horse was only wounded one time, and that was in the leg. He led his warriors to victory many times, and was victorious because he was not afraid to die. Today, we American Indians are still not afraid of our greatest natural enemy, *"death"*. American Indians have the highest suicide rate of any population in the world.

When American Indians come to the knowledge that God loves them very much, that they are ***extremely valuable and precious to God, and to the human race,*** they accept Jesus Christ as their Lord and Savior, and then allow the Great Holy Spirit to fill them with the evidence of speaking in God's supernatural language (as Acts 2:4 describes), they will rise up as the great warriors that God created them to be. They will fearlessly challenge satan's greatest forces of sickness, disease and physical death. They will not care what people say to them, or about them, because they know how to die to self, *"to pride"*. American Indians will command blinded eyes and deaf ears to open, and crippled and deformed bodies to be made instantly whole, right in the open public, right into the face of their greatest critics and opposition. Openly, they will walk into funeral processions, after people are already embalmed (like Jesus with Lazarus), and raise people from the dead.

A person must die to self image, self pride, and self ambition, to everything about self, if they want to see the fullness of God in operation in their lives. The Apostle Paul died daily to his pride and self (I Corinthians 15:31). Except for Jesus, Paul had more gifts of the Holy Spirit and miracles in operation in his life than any one in the Bible. American Indians are born with the characteristic of dying to self pride.

It does not mean we Indians are better than any one else, God just made us this way. For instance, a natural singer is born with the ability to sing.

American Indians love to dance their ancestral dances. We Indians do it as part of our genetic makeup. Since we are dancing to our Creator, and it gives us joy and strength, we are not embarrassed by our dancing. We Indians would never consider laughing or ridiculing some one that does not dance exactly like other people. We realize all people are individuals, and any dancer may perform the dance which expresses his individually in worshiping the Almighty.

The Scriptures tell us, where the Spirit of the Lord is, there is liberty (II Corinthians 3:17). I have held Miracle services in several other countries, and I usually have at least one service in which I teach the people to do the American Indian Dance of Thanksgiving. These services are always the largest services, and always the strongest. Nearly always in these dancing services, 100% of the people are on their feet and dancing. I always experience more people giving their lives to Christ, being born again, and having the highest percentage of Healings and Miracles during dancing services.

I can remember in Japan a couple of years ago, during the last service, we played Indian music and taught the people to dance the Dance of Thanksgiving. All of the people in that service began dancing for joy, except one lady. This lady was brought in on a stretcher, in the last stages of life. She was more dead than alive. No one prayed for her, or even spoke to her. After every one else had been dancing for about 10 minutes, she got herself up off her stretcher, and began dancing. She became healed by the love of God. There is power in dancing.

In Psalms 100:4, the Bible says we actually enter into the deepest presence of God by praise. This word **_praise_** in Psalms 100:4 is the Hebrew word **_tehillah_**, which is the highest order of praise in the Old Testament. The fuller meaning of this word is to celebrate, to be glamorously foolish in the praise of God. This word is used quite often in the Old Testament when dancing is involved. Dancing unto the Lord is **_tehillah_**; this will take a person in the deepest presence of God. II Corinthians 3:17, tells us that where the Spirit of the Lord is, there is liberty (freedom). When we dance with our whole hearts, as our ancestors did in the Ghost Dance, the Spirit of the Lord is then present in His highest order. There is liberty and freedom from sickness, disease, and poverty, and freedom from all of the approaches of satan. Dancing unto the Lord, as our Indian people did in the Ghost Dance, is most definitely dying to self.

The body of Christ needs the ministry and gifts of the American Indians.

CHAPTER 4

Big Forgivers

Forgiveness is the subject of the strongest passage in the Scriptures, Mark 11:24, 25. In the Indian mind, we are more interested in forgiving, and restoring a relationship, than we are in holding a grudge.

I can still remember seeing the look on my father's face when bitterness crept into a conversation. He would immediately turn the conversation to something that would cause laughter. Forgiveness, in the heart of the Indian, is something that is done long before it is ever desired from the transgressor. Unforgiveness destroys a life, or an atmosphere of joy. Romans 15:32 tells us, "If we come with joy, by the will of God, people will be refreshed". The will of God is that we forgive all people. Jesus taught His disciples to daily forgive their debtors. Debtors are people that owe us something. They may owe us an apology, money, or something else of value. Forgiveness is definitely the will of God. As we forgive, we create an atmosphere that is not natural, it is supernatural; it is a divine atmosphere of joy.

Forgiveness is an extremely powerful force. Not only does forgiveness allow Mark 11:24 to become a reality in a person's life, it is a power that will raise the dead. When Jesus was on the cross, He cried Father forgive them (Luke 23:34), and later Jesus rose from the dead (after being dead for 3 days and three nights).

I John 3:14 says, "We KNOW that we have passed from death (eternal spiritual death) unto life (life in this passage is the Greek word ***Zoë***, which is the ***God kind of life***), because we love the brethren". Forgiveness is proof that the love of God is in one's heart and they are a true child of GOD. We can KNOW we are children of God, with an eternal destiny of heaven, because we love people. I John 4:7, 8 tells us plainly that "Love is of God, and EVERYONE that loveth is born of God, and knoweth God". God says we are His children if we love. I John 4:8 says that "God is love". Verse 16 says "If we dwell (remain) in love, we dwell in God". Some people are not sure if they are going to heaven when they die. The Bible says we will KNOW we are going to heaven if we love.

A great Lakota Sioux warrior named Short Bull was discussed in Chapter 2. Active in teaching and preaching about the "Ghost Dance" movement, Short Bull had a vision of seeing the Messiah (Jesus Christ, the Son of the Living God). After his vision, Short Bull became a very kind and loving person. Pictures of Short Bull following his experience of seeing and talking with Jesus reflects a look of gentleness and kindness on his face. You can actually see the Shekina Glory on his countenance.

When the slaughter of Wounded Knee took place (December 29, 1890), twenty three of Short Bull's relatives where killed. He made the statement that he was tempted to take up a weapon and fight in defense of his relatives. However, he also said something like, "If I am angered, I am the worst among you. I have put all badness from me and want to be a good man. I want to do as the Messiah bid me. This message was given by the Father to all the tribes. For the message was of peace."

Note by Mel Bond - For any human to speak with such conviction, and exhibit such supernatural love as to forgive the people who slaughtered his loved ones, then he clearly has Divine impartation upon his life. Indians forgive by their God given nature. However, this forgiving nature is compounded when we are born again by accepting Jesus Christ as our Lord and Savior (Romans 10:9, 10).

When Columbus first came to our country, there were at least 9 to 12 million Indians in America. Some scholars place the number as high as 40 million Indians. According to the U.S. census, there were only about 250,000 Indians remaining in America by 1900. Keep in mind; many babies were born during this 400 year period. Clearly, there were many millions of our people destroyed.

Most of the American Indians were destroyed by diseases, imported from foreign countries, for which their bodies had no natural immunity. Obviously, if immigrants had not migrated to our country, this tragedy would not have occurred. As medical treatment evolved, it was routinely withheld from the American Indian.

There was millions of American Indians slaughtered in hideous ways by the European whites. When you read books like "Bury My Heart at Wounded Knee" by Dee Brown, books written about the Trail of Tears, and books by Dr. Charles Alexander Eastman (Ohiyesa), you will learn about horrible torturing of our people. It has been stated that Adolph Hitler learned his torturing techniques from the way American Indians were tortured.

Many Christians criticize American Indians by saying, "Why don't they (American Indians) just forgive and go on with life". As a born again, God loving Indian, I whole heartedly agree. However, I would like to submit two comments for your consideration. First, assume your grandparents were multi-trillionaires, and your neighbor stole everything they had, they made you live in poverty, took your name, your identity, and tortured your ancestors beyond imagination. Would you be able to forgive your neighbor? Secondly, without a divine spirit, no one can forgive on a divine level. A divine spirit only comes from being born again and by accepting Jesus Christ as your Lord and Savior. Another fact that needs to be considered is, "NOBODY cares what you know, until they know that you care". American Indians will accept Jesus Christ as their Lord and Savior when the actions of love come to them from true Christians. American Indians need to know that they are just as valuable and precious as any other race. Indians need a flood of God's love toward them, and that comes through true Christians.

In spite of the destruction of the American Indian, our people still forgave, helped, and loved the immigrants (intruders), and accepted them as their own. In the Indian mind, forgiveness is also forgetting, and loving unconditionally. Forgiving in this magnitude can only be accomplished by

God's great love in a person's heart. Jesus said, "That ye love one another, as I have loved you, that ye also love one another. By this shall all men know that ye are my disciples, if ye have love one to another (John 13:34, 35)". Keep in mind that God is Love (I John 4:7, 8; 16). Forgiveness is the true test of God living in a person's heart. Forgiveness is the true test of knowing you are a child of God. (I John 3:14, "We KNOW we have passed from death to life, because we Love"!)

It was 1915 when Short Bull told of Jesus' (the Messiah) appearing and standing in the middle of a group of Ghost Dancers. Jesus stood with His head bowed, and all at once, surprisingly, He made a speech in the Lakota language. He said, "Because you come to me suffering, you will hear those things that are right, and you will act accordingly. By means of a dance, you will see again those of your relatives who died long ago; but only if you do it properly will you truly see your people. I was killed long ago by the white men, and now there are many holes in me. The holes went away, and now they honor me. You Indian people are suffering and I am paying you this visit so, in the future, you and your relatives who have died, will see one another. From this time on, by dancing and doing those things that I will tell you, you will live well. My beloved son, do not murder one another! Whoever commits murder does evil. Love one another! Take pity on one another! If you act in this manner, I will give you more concerning the ceremony."

If you do research on the Ghost Dance, you will find that Wovoka was one of the first Indian people to see Jesus. On the first visitation of Jesus, Wovoka looked at Jesus' hands, and asked why He did not have any scars in the palms of

His hands (the European whites told Wovoka that Jesus was crucified and hung on the cross with nails through the palms of His hands). Jesus told him that He was not pierced in the palms of his hands, but in His wrists. Jesus then rolled up his sleeves and showed Wovoka the terrible scars in his wrists. This action validates that Jesus did in fact appear to our people in the Ghost Dance, since only recently have scholars validated that Jesus was crucified in His wrists.

Forgiveness is most definitely a major characteristic that God requires of people to perform His last day's greatest work on earth. American Indians are born with the characteristic of forgiveness in their hearts. Imagine what is going to happen when thousands of our people allow God's forgiveness to be compounded with the forgiveness that we are born with.

In Joel 2:2, God says there is a last day's people that will come forth that will be "A great and strong (powerful) people. Their like has never been before, nor will be again after them." Verse 3 says that "Nothing shall escape this people". Nothing means *nothing*. They will take authority over all sicknesses, disease, poverty and even physical death. No enemy shall escape them. Verse 10 says, "The earth shall quake before them; the heavens shall tremble". Verse 11 says, "The Lord shall say this is His army". Notice in Joel 2:7, 8, in the midst of all these powerful statements, God says "They will not break their ranks. They will never trust another". Unforgiveness causes division, and it is a deep wound into the eternal spirit of a person. However, this last day's people will be American Indians (and like minded people) who are great forgivers.

In I John 1:9, the Bible tells us, "If we confess our sins,

He (God) is faithful and just to FORGIVE us our sins, and to cleanse us from all unrighteousness". When God forgives, He co-equally cleanses and purifies to the point where the transgression never existed. The true characteristic of American Indians is exactly the same. This is another reason why God is going to use American Indians (and like minded people) for His last day's greatest move.

CHAPTER 5

Humility

In general, American Indians are very polite, gentle, and soft spoken. As a result, the Indian population as a whole, and especially men, are mistakenly considered to be a weak people. Often times, the men are even thought to be feminine (a sissy), due to our very mild and humble dispositions. However, when the time arrives for a man or a great warrior to appear on the scene, like Clark Kent turning into Superman, the bystanders are amazed and shocked to see the transformation of what appears to be a weak and timid man into a fierce and powerful warrior.

When you read Charles Eastman's (Ohiyesa) books, you will find him telling stories of some of the greatest Indian warriors using this same exact description. Born in February 1858, Ohiyesa was a Santee Sioux (also known as the Dakota). He received and used the white man's name Charles Alexander Eastman to gain acceptance by the white people. Ohiyesa was raised and educated as a young man in the ancient ways of the Dakota. Ohiyesa later attended, and was educated in, some of the best white man's schools in the world, going on to become a medical doctor. His first job was as a physician for the Indian Agency at Pine Ridge, South Dakota. Dr. Charles Alexander Eastman (Ohiyesa) was the medical doctor for the Indian people that survived the massacre at Wounded Knee on December 29, 1890. I provide this information about Ohiyesa to validate his intelligence and his knowledge of the ancient ways of the Indian people.

In ancient times, as well as today, we Indian people exhibit politeness in our homes. It was quite common for our greatest warriors to treat his family and friends with the greatest of gentleness and tenderness. A soft, low voice was considered an excellent quality in a man (as well as women and children).

Jesus said in Matthew 18:4, "Whosoever therefore shall humble himself as this little child, the same is greatest in the kingdom of heaven". One of the co-equal words for humility in the Hebrew language is gentleness. If we have true, pure humility, it will be in our every day life. It will be exhibited in places where no one can see, or know, of the demonstration of humility. When humility is real in one's private life, then there is an undeniable, eternal, divine manifestation of humility in the company of people. The demonstration of humility is not a show, it is a glow. It is not for promotion or recognition by others, but rather it is a privilege that allows one to walk with the Creator of all existence.

I have raised animals all of my life, and I have found that the Indian ways to tame an animal work the best. You can break a wild horse to a gentle, dependable horse by exercising a lot of gentleness and patience during the training of the horse. I have raised elk since 1992 and I have found that by being gentle, I can gain their confidence. The technique works so well that I can even perform the most difficult tasks without help or assistance from others. The elk simply follow after me like tame little dogs. I routinely perform most of the artificial insemination procedures without any assistance.

HUMILITY OF JESUS

Humility was a strong characteristic of Jesus. In Philippians 2:7, 8, the Bible says in verse 7, "But made himself of no reputation, and took upon him the form of a servant, and was made in the likeness of men". In verse 8, "And being found in fashion as a man, he humbled himself, and became obedient unto death, even the death of the cross". Jesus seemed to appear weak and fragile, and always conducted himself with gentleness. He became the greatest of all warriors by conquering the greatest enemy of mankind – physical death. He was beat beyond recognition as a human being and he never complained or retaliated one time. Three days and three nights after His death, Jesus rose from the dead.

James 4:10, tells us to "Humble yourself in the sight of the Lord and He shall lift you up". Humility is a strong characteristic that God highly honors. Humility, demonstrated in the life of a human, is ground that God will promote, and no one can deny or take it away. Proverbs 18:12, tells us that "Before honor is humility". Chapter 2 of Philippians provides instructions to allow humility to rule in our lives, and then it tells us plainly in verse 5 to "Let this mind be in you that was also in Christ Jesus". Verse 6 says, "Who being in the form of God, thought it not robbery to be equal with God".

Humility is another great characteristic in Indian people, and this is another reason why God is going to use them for the greatest work he has ever done on the earth. Indians (and like minded people) will become equal with God, not as God Almighty (as any true Christian has no desire in the slightest to be in that position). However, the truth being validated here is the truth that coincides with the rest of the Bible and that is that God wants us to be equal with him in authority over the devil and all of the demonic forces. He wants us to have authority over all sickness, disease, poverty and even physical death. The Bible says that physical death is the last enemy that shall be destroyed (I Corinthians 15; 26). When we Indians get into the right place where God wants us, we will raise people from the dead (that have been embalmed and dead), so that the Father may be highly glorified (John 14:12-14).

I speak to all of the Indian people and say, be encouraged and continue to let God's Divine humility rule in your lives. Wakantanka is about to lift us up!

Jesus said in Matthew 19:30 that, "The first shall be last; and the last shall be first". Indian people are the least recognized people in the world. We are a race of people that were almost totally destroyed. We are a race of people having the smallest population in the world. We have not tried to push our way for our rights or to be recognized. It is simply not our nature to do so. However, this is another reason why God is going to use American Indians (and like minded people) in the last days for His greatest work.

I Peter 5:6 says, "Humble yourselves therefore under the mighty hand of God, that he may exalt you in due time". In the Greek, the word for *time* is exactly the same word for *time* in I Peter 1:5 where God says he has an inheritance that is reserved in heaven, a salvation ready to be revealed in the last time. This word *time* is also co-equally rendered *season*. I am convinced that God has a special, literal season of the greatest thing he has ever done on this earth. American Indians (and like minded people) will be the principle participants that he will entrust with such a divine task.

CHAPTER 6

Indians Are Givers

When Columbus first came to America, he was surprised by the manner in which the American Indian people greeted their group and treated them with extreme kindness. When Columbus returned to Europe, the Europeans ask him about the Indian people. He told them that the Indian people were the kindest and most giving people that he had ever met. He told the Europeans that the Indians gave him and his crew their most valuable personal possessions as gifts. In that period of time, the American Indians made valuable jewelry, and handed it down from generation to generation. In this way, their jewelry not only had monetary valuable, but had tremendous sentimental value. Columbus stated that the American Indian people took the jewelry off their necks and gave it to him and his crew members.

The Europeans ask Columbus about American Indian laws, how lawbreakers were prosecuted, and what Indian jails were like. Columbus replied that there were no American Indian jails because no Indians broke the law. The Indian nature is not to take (steal) from anyone. If someone wanted an object belonging to someone else, they had only to ask for it, and it would be joyfully given to them. American Indian values are eternal and spiritual, not temporal or earthly. The character of the American Indian people is that there is no reason to steal, lie, cheat, or kill.

In the American Indian language, there are no curse words. We Indians give only those words that would be uplifting and encouraging to people. One of the highest characteristics of God is giving. God so loved the world that He gave the very best he had – his son (John 3:16).

SHORT BULL

When you read material spoken by Short Bull, as well as other material written about him, you will find that he was willing often times to lay down his life for his people in battle. However, after he experienced a vision of Jesus daily for 5 days during a Ghost Dance, his life changed dramatically. Jesus told Short Bull to tell the Indian people to work the ground and go to church. Jesus told him that all over the world, everyone is just like the other, and no distinction should be made. He also told Short Bull to always sing and pray about Him (Jesus).

When Short Bull returned to the Rosebud Reservation (following his visitation with Jesus during the Ghost Dance), he began telling others of the things that Jesus had told him; how it was a life changing experience and how it would change everyone's life who would obey the words of Jesus. The Rosebud Reservation Agents had Short Bull arrested, and questioned him concerning the Ghost Dance. Short Bull told the agents about Jesus, and everything that

Short Bull a Sioux Indian 1845-1915.

He fought at the battle of Big Horn. After Jesus Christ appeared to him about 1890 before the Massacre at Wounded Knee he brought the Ghost Dance to the Lakota's.

had happened at the Ghost Dance. The Agents told Short Bull that he would be killed if he told this information to the Indian people. Short Bull told the Agents they might as well pick up a gun and shoot him because he felt it was necessary to share the words of Jesus with his people. Short Bull was not being arrogant by what he said to the Rosebud Reservation Agents; he was just willing to give his life for the betterment of his people. In those days, it was suicide for an Indian to talk to a Reservation Government Agent like Short Bull did. An Indian's life meant very little, and many times they would be shot dead for simply not saying just exactly what an Agent wanted to hear. To better understand this concept, I will provide you with some information about Standing Bear.

STANDING BEAR OF THE PONCAS TRIBE

On April 18, 1879, Standing Bear was in litigation with the courts of the United States of America to prove that Indians were human beings. Standing Bear provided testimony in court before Judge Dundy. "Almighty God looks upon me, and He knows what I am. The Almighty God hears my words and prayers. I pray that the Almighty God would send a good spirit to come over you, that you would be influenced by His goodness to help me. I ask you to please have mercy on me, help me to save myself and the lives of the women and children. My brothers, a power, which I cannot resist, crowds me down to the earth and I need help."

As a victorious result of this now almost forgotten civil rights litigation known as Standing Bear vs. Crook, Standing Bear and American Indians throughout the United States were declared human beings by the United States

Government. From the litigation of Standing Bear vs. Crook you can understand that the life of the Indian meant very little, as Indians were not considered human.

So now you can understand when Short Bull spoke as he did to the Rosebud agent it meant death for him. Short Bull's courageous testimony declared his willingness to lay down his life so that others could have a better way of life through Jesus Christ (Romans 10:9, 10).

WOUNDED KNEE MASSACRE AND STILL GIVING UNCONDITIONAL LOVE

On December 29, 1890, 350 Lakota Sioux people (120 men 230 women, children, and babies), under Chief Big Foot's leadership, where surrounded by approximately 500 well armed combat troops of the 7th U.S. Calvary. During the attempt to disarm the warriors, a Lakota rifle was accidentally discharged. Most of the Indian people were totally unarmed (not even a knife as a weapon) but the 7th U.S. Cavalry soldiers quickly discharged their Hotchkiss guns and rifles on the defenseless Indians. There were twenty some medal of honors awarded to various soldiers for slaughtering those helpless Indian men, women, children, and babies.

The next day, Short Bull went to the sight of the massacre and gave the following account. Short Bull said he found one of his uncles who had been horribly shot in the leg, but was still alive. His uncle told Short Bull that all of the Indians had their guns and knives taken from them (there were only about 20 guns, and most of them were pieces of junk). As Short Bull's uncle went into his tent to get his knife to surrender it, the firing began, and he was shot in the leg.

His uncle had laid there since the battle the previous day.

Short Bull found twenty three of his own relatives lying there dead. The dead consisted of men, women and children. Short Bull said it was butchery. He said he was tempted to take up weapons and fight in defense of his people. Short Bull could have easily armed himself and charged into battle because he had been in many battles, and was known as a great warrior. However, Short Bull exercised restraint and said he was not looking for trouble, but if he was angered he would be considered the worst among them. Short Bull said he removed all evil from himself, and wanted to be a good man. He said he wanted to do as the Messiah told him. Short Bull was told by Jesus, "Behold, I am telling you something for you to tell to all the people! Tell all people to dance and worship together. Stop fighting! Stop killing! Love one another. Help one another. Do not sin against anyone."

THE HIGHEST TEST OF GIVING

Short Bull, a seasoned Lakota Sioux warrior, had the greatest test that any human could have. He saw his family butchered, and saw his uncle lying in deep snow and extreme cold weather. However, instead of harboring feelings of retaliation and evil, Short Bull *gave forgiveness*. Jesus said in John 15:13, "Greater love hath no man than this man lay down his life for his friends". In this verse, the word *friend* is co-equally rendered *neighbor*. The word *love* is exactly the same word for love in I John 4:8, where it says that "*God is love*".

There is no greater proof of God in one's life than to lay down their life for a neighbor. Short Bull did exactly that, many times in his life. He was willing to lay down his anger, pride, and revenge, and act like a true child of God. No person can do this by human strength. This behavior can only be demonstrated by a person that has had a true encounter with the Great God of all.

LUKE 6:38

Most of the time, references to Luke 6:38 are used to show God's blessing on the financial giver. However, there is a much greater truth about giving in Luke, Chapter 6. In verse 35, Jesus tells us if we follow the Scriptures in Chapter 6 we would be the children of the Highest (which is of God). We shall now look at the verses in Chapter 6 which will enable us to be the children of God.

In verse 27, "Love your enemies, and do good to them which hate you". This word *love* is exactly the same Greek word for love in I John 4:8, where it says that ***God is Love***. So we are supposed to deposit God into our enemy's lives and to those that hate us. This word *love* is also an ***unconditional love.***

In verse 28, "Bless them that curse you, and pray for them which despitefully use you".

In verse 29, "And unto him that smiteth thee on the one cheek, offer also the other; and him that taketh away thy cloke, forbid not to take thy coat also".

In verse 30, "Give to every man that asketh of thee; and of him that taketh away thy goods ask them not again".

(Note - This may seem extremely harsh and unfair. However, if you justify yourself, you will get self justification.

However, if God justifies you, you will have God's supernatural justification. This supernatural justification will be compounded beyond what you could imagine (Ephesians 3:19).

In verse 32, "For if ye love them which love you, what thank have ye? For sinners also love those that love them".

In verse 35, "But love ye your enemies, and do good, and lend, hoping for nothing again; and your reward shall be great; and YE SHALL BE THE CHILDREN OF THE HIGHEST! For he is kind (the Greek word for *kind* is co-equally rendered = *good, gracious and furnishes what is needed*) unto the unthankful and to the evil".

Indians, for hundreds of years, have practiced Luke, Chapter 6. This is a major reason that Wakantanka is going to use American Indians (and like minded people) for His grand finale.

Speaking God's Word makes you sound like God. Giving God's Unconditional Love to others makes you like God.

CHAPTER 7

Indians Are People Of Integrity

The word ***integrity*** in the Hebrew language of the Old Testament is also rendered ***truth.*** Most dictionaries will also render it as ***honesty***.

We American Indians are people of our words. Our words are better than any man made contract. When I was growing up, my father started a septic tank business. I went with him many times to help clean out a customer's septic tank, and I never saw him write a contract. My father would always explain the terms and conditions of his work to the customer, and then he just shook hands with the customer.

Ecclesiastes 5:5 says, "Better is it that thou shouldest not ***vow*** (The Hebrew renders this word also as ***promise***), than that thou shouldest vow and not ***pay*** (the Hebrew word co-equally is rendered ***complete, make good***)". There is a curse that comes on people that are not good for their word.

ELVEN BOND

As the years went by, my father started a plumbing company which was much more complex and involved than the septic tank business. The plumbing company provided much more opportunity in which to be taken advantage. However, all the times I worked with my father in the plumbing company, I never saw him write a contract. We installed all of the plumbing in new homes based on a hand shake. Many times people took advantage of us. We worked in the mud of basements, sometimes at least a foot deep, digging the sewer systems by hand. The work was extremely hard. There were times that we put all of the plumbing in a new home, and we would end up paying for some of the material and receive no labor compensation because people would take advantage of my father's integrity. However, Proverbs 19:1 ruled on the behalf of my father, "Better is the poor that walketh in his integrity, than he that is perverse (false) in his lips, and is a fool".

There is something so supernaturally satisfying about laying your head down at night and knowing you have done an honest days work, even though it may have cost you dearly. On the inside of Indians, there is deep concern that we live up to the guarantees we make, and we will do what we said we will do. It is stamped on our hearts. It hurts Indians more not to keep their word, than it could ever possibly hurt the person to whom we gave our word.

It was very obvious that my father worked extremely hard, as if each job were being done for God himself. I will never forget digging the ditches for the sewer systems in homes. My father would not allow each ditch to be anything less than perfect. Each ditch would be perfectly straight. Each wall and floor of each ditch would be a perfect 90 degree angle. It took us three times longer to dig the *perfect* ditch; and it seemed to be senseless and a waste of time and energy. However, to my father, it was as if each ditch was being dug for Jesus. In Colossians 3:23, the Bible says, "Whatsoever ye do, do it heartily, as to the Lord, and not unto men".

When we were working in the septic tank business, I can remember a sewage line would occasionally spray raw sewage in my father's face and across his mouth. He would wipe it off and laugh about it. Most people would have cursed and found another job. However, if it was unto the Lord, it is absolutely OK.

As I mentioned earlier, my father was a perfectionist, and he felt motivated to dig the perfect sewer ditch. It was not necessary to put the sewers in a perfect ditch. A simple ditch, that was basically straight, with the contour of a shovel, would allow the sewer system to work just fine. Even the sewer inspectors did not care how perfect the ditch was. Only the inspector would see the ditches (and God). But my father's integrity caused him to be a man of an excellent spirit. It caused him to be a man you could trust with your life. You could trust my father to do what he said he would do, even if he knew you would never inspect his word or work. Jesus said in Luke 16:10, "He that is faithful in that which is least, is faithful also in much: and he that is unjust (untrustworthy) in the least, is unjust also in much". In Proverbs 20:7, "The just man walketh in his integrity: his children are blessed after him".

The Lord has allowed me to enjoy great prosperity because

of the integrity of my Father. I have been supernaturally aware that my father's presence has worked in the *office of an angel* (Luke 20:36; Matthew 22:30) to cause my goals and ambitions to come to pass. After my father passed away, within a couple of months I started to notice his presence in helping me in many ways. Once I even noticed his presence in saving my life.

Proverbs 20:7 says, "The righteous person behaves in integrity; blessed are his children". This Scripture has become very true for me. My father was always extremely happy when his children were blessed. All of his children where, and are, more financially blessed than he ever imagined for himself. There was never the slightest hint of jealousy, but instead my father had only a deep gratitude to the Creator for his children being blessed. This is the integrity of an American Indian. This is the integrity that is Godly.

My father lived in relative poverty most of his life, but that was OK with him. As with all American Indians, we know that the greatest riches are riches that no man or demonic forces can take away from us. The true riches of God are of the spirit. Romans 14; 17 says, "For the kingdom of God is not meat and drink; (not natural things) but righteousness, and peace, and joy in the Holy Ghost".

Proverbs 20:7, tells us the just man walketh in his integrity: his children are blessed after him. My father never knew that God wanted to honor him, not just spiritually and mentally, but also financially. Therefore, my father never trusted God for great financial riches. However, because of the integrity of God in my mother and father's life, I have dedicated my life to God and His Word. I have determined that it is a great desire of God to cause financial blessings upon his children. (III John 2;4; Psalm 35:27 as well as a host of other Scriptures). The foundation of all divine prosperity is Deuteronomy 8:18, "Remember the Lord thy God; for it is He that giveth thee power to get wealth, that He may establish His covenant, which He swore unto thy fathers".

CROW DOG

When you study the life of Chief Crow Dog, a Lakota Sioux Indian, you will find a story to validate the great integrity of the American Indian people. Crow Dog was imprisoned in South Dakota about 1881 and was sentenced to be executed. A few days before his execution date, Crow Dog asked permission to go home and bid farewell to his wife and twin boys. Although totally unusual, his request was granted with the escort of a deputy sheriff. For some reason, the deputy sheriff decided to stay at the Indian agency, and told Chief Crow Dog to go see his family by himself and report back to the agency on the following day. Chief Crow Dog did not show up at the appointed time, so the sheriff dispatched the Indian police to go find him. As the Indian police arrived at the home of Crow Dog, they determined that he was gone. Chief Crow Dog's wife told the Indian police that Crow Dog left earlier that day because he wanted to ride to the prison alone. Crow Dog instructed his wife to tell anyone looking for him that he would be at the prison on the appointed day and time. The next day, Rapid City (which was about 200 miles away) sent a telegram indicating that Crow Dog had just reported in.

How many people in this world would lie and cheat just to make a few dollars? From the beginning of our American

Indian culture, lying was considered a capital offense among us. We believe that a person who is a deliberate liar is capable of committing any crime. Jesus said the same thing in different words in Matthew 12:43-45, "When an unclean spirit leaves a person, and then comes back, that evil spirit will bring with him, into that person's life, seven other evil spirits, much worse than the first unclean spirit."

To uphold integrity, even if it costs you your life, is proof of the highest degree of Godly integrity possible. True Godly integrity takes a person beyond any self preservation. As you study true American Indian history, you will find hundreds of stories like that of Chief Crow Dog. I would venture to guess that there are thousands, if not millions of stories like Chief Crow Dog which have only been recorded in the heart of Wakantanka (Almighty God).

I am very convinced that American Indians (and like minded people) are who God wants to use in His last day's work. However, all prophecy is conditional. If we accept the conditions of the prophecy, it will happen. God will not make any one do something they do not want to. The highest order of prophecy is God's Word. The highest mandate or prophecy of God, is that no human should perish, but that all should come to repentance (II Peter 3:10). It is very clear that God's will is His highest order of prophecy, and His will is that none perish, but that all accept Jesus Christ as their Lord.